THE PORTAG

SERIES TITLES

Not Just the Fire
R.B. Simon

Monarch
Heather Bourbeau

The Walk to Cefalù
Lynne Viti

The Found Object Imagines a Life: New and Selected Poems
Mary Catherine Harper

Naming the Ghost
Emily Hockaday

Mourning
Dokubo Melford Goodhead

Messengers of the Gods: New and Selected Poems
Kathryn Gahl

After the 8-Ball
Colleen Alles

Careful Cartography
Devon Bohm

Broken On the Wheel
Barbara Costas-Biggs

Sparks and Disperses
Cathleen Cohen

Holding My Selves Together: New and Selected Poems
Margaret Rozga

Lost and Found Departments
Heather Dubrow

Marginal Notes
Alfonso Brezmes

The Almost–Children
Cassondra Windwalker

Meditations of a Beast
Kristine Ong Muslim

There's a gorgeous intersection of lyricism and the laconic...
with lines so good they scream-whisper. Gouirand's voice is
hypnotic and potent.

—Natalie Eilbert

Rae: lexical powerhouse. Rae: scientist of intimacies. The words
burst as though the poet could not contain them.

—Thylias Moss

Her capacity for eloquence is as vast as her rhetoric is supple.

—Raymond McDaniel

Hers is a new music, indeed a new order of language altogether.

—Richard Howard

Rae Gouirand's [*Glass is Glass Water is Water*] continues the
tradition of poetry by lesbians adumbrating lesbian experience
into US politics. Gouirand's poems about ambivalence toward
marriage in the post-Obergefell world continue this work with
exquisite beauty and insight.

—Julie Enszer

There is something comparable to Anne Carson in how
Gouirand approaches writing the physical, sensual, and sexual
self, and her connection to both a lover and to language itself: 'It
is incredibly important to draw lines around words.' Gouirand's
work...can't easily be described but only absorbed.

—Rob McClellan

If Adrienne Rich wrote prose, it would come out something like this. This work is more powerful to me than *Twenty-One Love Poems* and that. is. saying. a. lot.

—Lidia Yuknavitch

The History of Art is wide open, complex, dirty, clean, revelatory, and flat-out amazing.

—Daniel Mahoney

We join the speaker's body in these pages. We meet her at the vanishing point. We too find our missing skin. So many lines of these essays peak and resound, unmaking and awakening, but this queer femme erotic is not only about artifice destroyed but also a lyric of the parts that cannot be summarized, the body's pre-verbal spaces. Gouirand writes of meeting the hunger of this queer dissatisfaction, of accessing and serving a queer body's need to be a work of her own making.

—Barrie Jean Borich

Gouirand pushes at gaps, from the chasms words create (that which uttering them and composing them renders in the body, heart) to the inevitable ruptures of coupling (both in love and in the syntactical act of joining signifier to signified). There is light and potential in these gaps. It's hard to describe these poems adequately in a single way, hard to describe the strange miracle of this poet's work without flattening the experience or launching into philosophical outer space. In reading her, I understand in my body and am moved. My brain is piqued and my ear hums. In writing her, I lack the right words.

—Rachel Mindell

THE
VELVET
BOOK

RAE GOUIRAND

CORNERSTONE PRESS
UNIVERSITY OF WISCONSIN-STEVENS POINT

Cornerstone Press, Stevens Point, Wisconsin 54481
Copyright © 2024 Rae Gouirand
www.uwsp.edu/cornerstone

Printed in the United States of America by
Point Print and Design Studio, Stevens Point, Wisconsin

Library of Congress Control Number: 2024935795
ISBN: 978-1-960329-37-0

Cornerstone Press titles are produced in courses and internships offered by the
Department of English at the University of Wisconsin–Stevens Point.

DIRECTOR & PUBLISHER
Dr. Ross K. Tangedal

EXECUTIVE EDITORS
Jeff Snowbarger, Freesia McKee

EDITORIAL DIRECTOR
Ellie Atkinson

SENIOR EDITORS
Brett Hill, Grace Dahl

PRESS STAFF
Carolyn Czerwinski, Sophie McPherson, Eva Nielsen, Natalie Reiter, Ava Willett

we were like that then—
Jammed wrong & wrong in the diurnal

Mangy chambers of our carnall
Hearts, the rose robes rustling loose as velvet

Curtains at the stage prow

—Lucie Brock-Broido, "Carnivorous"

Remember me: wishing, specific, marooned, as
One who knew exactly what the Ever was & is, a velvet school
Of courtesan, a gallows bird, all deep, all deepening.

—Lucie Brock-Broido, "Still Life With Aspirin"

The diagnosis is not possible

Before the Posthumous. Don't pout.
    What animal, do you think,
Would velvet be the pelt of?

            —Lucie Brock-Broido, "Fame Rubies"

Seering flare for deeper pitch,
flashbulb for sudden ink, stress for disintegration

for the glint that erupts—
dazzle to curse to rupture to rush

changing pulse, simultaneous,
each new to the other. Each a change.

If I vowed I would speak
all words at once. All the speakable words

after a silence as long as all
the unspeakable words lined up one by one like

a line. Words are all words
at once. Silences one word at a time.

At a time is the life of velvet.
I am relentless remembering it,

scribbled across my own pile.
Face or stain I cannot choose. Each learns,

each leans. I am my own body
inside this, finishing. I make myself available

as a hunger would for naming.
Velvet for the structure not the fiber.

The reach of the surface toward
every mote floating. Is it any matter

we say *fabric of the time* as it blinks,
shakes, shimmers, climbs behind the drapes.

See it there climbing.
Most of the time since its invention

we've preferred something else
yet the pull asserts, late August on a plane

a heavy white spine glossed against
the thigh, the start of a dream about cold, about

color, about puncture, about capture
by one unable to look away from the deep

and deepening folds of the coat
saturated ahead of us. Velvet how deep

we soak, how hard we press
the pen, how thoroughly we test

the argument. The whole of it.
Is it bright ahead? Enthusiastic? Yes and dark.

From Old Provençal via vulgar Latin
diminutive of shaggy cloth, nap of cloth, tuft

of hair, *vellus*, fleece, suffixed form of
*wel to tear, to pull, see *svelte* which evokes

lengthened, pulled, plucked. A certain kind
of night. I've read a little of velvet transparent,

breath held for air liased through it.
Devoré, burned out. Embossed, hammered,

mirror velvet, nacré like shot silk
its iridescence bolts in two directions at once,

pile on pile, Utrecht, voided, and
wedding ring, a chiffon type fine enough

to be drawn through that blinking.
All catalogued, like that shade of just-past violet

as night snaps. *Velvet is back*
the announcement. Arguing the pile,

the plush, the tongue upon
the back. Some suggestion of a likening,

the loops of the warp thread
left exposed. The soft, deciduous covering

of a growing antler
copper umber and lawn. Sixteen I was night.

When I reached back I felt
my path advance. Thought of what always meant.

That fruition. Lucre. Gravy.
Beetles' shades flying. Everything raised

the only question towards what.
Again and again short fibers between sense

and sensing. Where does
out start. What is velvet but:

before the limit something begins.
The territory is reactive and it is real.

Before the clock, before the gun.
I spend my life testing the opposite direction

with the very tip
of my existence. Me the field entered.

No question marks
for there is something beyond the ask.

It touches me everywhere even
in leaving, even when I drop my leaves.

In the moment we are woven,
the dark part where something leaves

something else behind.
Velvet when you are bending

the rules of light
first pitch, then phosphorous.

Cutting a slit through all of this.
What I'm looking for shifting into my fingers

in search of curtains to part.
I just cannot with the static sometimes.

It builds up & I wanna spark out.
When I speak I speak for myself. I rule;

I do not ribbon. What is that dominion?
I occupy this series of threads keeping neat.

Why even talk about the I—
inside there is space continuous with all space

except my defense has,
to a degree, survived. I am

warmest alone, dropped
into the texture of my yielding:

what doesn't bolt and bolt
then run out screaming about consent—

a welling collective and vague
it has a nap. The word *velvety* its own pile

meaning *smooth like velvet.*
I am trying to figure out what

beautiful things want—not
stillness, not immovability, though

I fix. Not
achievement, though I forbid

my absence
feeling something press.

Velvet the image I rehearsed
in the desert: a girl of redwood & lilac dust

spilled atop the bleached ground
for the long summer reading a worn paperback,

bedhead over elbows
by night her brutal cobalts and olives

under that mossy brown jacketing
the field. The sky lightning storms at noon,

chartreuse-winged birds swaying
in lavender while thunder shook teeth apart.

Velvet on a borrowed bed
thinking of horizons & sun-fired bone,

eyes rolled back & robins' eggs
on long arroyo walks like opals bezeled.

Velvet the alphabet of
clarity and will, how easily the hand pushed

brown ink between
mauve covers that nubuck a skin promised

a self. A woman sitting
at a rough table in a plain white shirt

caught just at the moment of looking
up from the book, its type just slightly wobbly

in the way of old type,
taking the eye offline for the space between

the letters, the even transparency
there, the solid standing wall upon which

every line ever written
glows through what one person once wrote.

Velvet was someone saying yes,
the room beyond this door, the space

between your ribs, where
between rib and rib darkness holds itself

compact as a line pressed from
the white. Velvet was the heaving, always

closing what could not stay open:
we were supposed to die out. / You had your face

pressed up against the coarse dyed velvet /
Of the curtain, always looking out for your own

transmigration: / What colors you would
wear, what cut of jewel posed the one whose lines

my hands horizoned.
So many kinds of pages.

If yellowing were the room
I'd think it art, but the books I've taught

lately seem lighter when I hold them,
as though their insides have burned off, as though

reminders, not the same things at all
as what I taught. We stopped embossing

once we'd memorized that
feeling of covers held. I rehearse it the way

I rehearse sleep, *mine*—
silken cherry & bronze pooled,

the honey tail of a snake winding up
a skirt walking into the dark, neon geometries,

a dress labradorite or marine teal,
pantlegs cropped cognac above the ankle,

a lounge so greenish-brackish it's
almost lost, a stack of albums furred in

celadon, emerald, moss, avocado,
celery, topaz, & fawn. All ribbons unwinding

hues across axes, all envelopes bearing
turkey feather, toadstool, slack dusk umber wilder

on the liner. Millinery flower
richer than the season it proclaims.

Goldenrod forward
for the street, chairs graduating

sherbet honeydew thyme lime
mallard, skylight powder wine the line

of seats. Could I put my life forward
skirt over tights. The headboard swallows gilt

for another fire, the jewelry box
warns of the weight of dark waters.

The window calms out.
Everything I touch goes wet. No revision

upon which to hang
a simple a-line garment. No neat shoulders

for a jacket cut neat in marigold,
small ribs for a buttoned line in coquelicot.

Dressing take it.
I want to sleep as one who has

escaped, want to swim in
something, an endlessness my skin

experiences, my cells deduce.
What is liquid for us, what will give us

us, what will break into
sensation and sensation again.

The minimalist gives up her point
of focus, drops her shoulders. All this

seeking. It's not just
the name I realize that should appear

only once. It's the whole girl.
Each should feel at some point

a separateness. In an instant's
flicker, a holograph a mirage a refracted edge

a double exposure déjà vu
silksheen shot through a subtle rayon,

trained, behaving—
as though a look can look back

the way we need to be looked at.
I have always slept eyes open, felt

more aperture.
Felt most information doesn't

belong. It changes the hand
running over it then the reading of that hand.

Once I was the thousand boxes
for the thousand palms. O Victoire,

o Norah, o Evey, o Blaire
o Blaire o Blaire o Blaire, your monograms

curl like a ribbon at the nape
around the neck to rest against

the thrump. What a laugh to say
lined with when velvet renders inside out.

O Audra, o Iris, o Mae,
I kept imagining your hands on it—

o Delilah, Corinne, Gloria,
Greta Greta your caterpillar scrawl Greta,

o Hazel a grand-diagonal mother's
mother, o Myrtle, o Octavia you raven-winged

blinker, o Quinnie, o Waverly
I am eavesdropping, I am dropped.

That visible kink
the moment's light catching us,

a bend a shine a road
rooted in thread rising toward wind,

toward what can be tempted.
The read of silver, of gold, of glint caught,

of hunted clamped, of thirst
announced. All the beauty the most thrown.

If dreaming of velvet
ask whether it is true or not.

I've gone down on every last
one of them, minus one. Velvet's a sense.

Childhood was a question
about what colors meant. Some dim,

others arrogant. Roses throated,
teethed. I looked a long time; the underside

pulsed: *Am lean against. / Am*
the heavy hour // Hand at urge, / At

the verge of one. Am the ice comb of
the tonsured // Hair, am the second / Hand, halted,

the velvet opera glove. Am slant. Am
fen, the injure // Wind at withins, / Stranger where

the storm forms a face if the body stands
enough // In a weather this / Cripple & this rough.

That *am* a coat, an *own.*
Velvety, meaning endowed.

Expensive, meaning backed.
Velvety meaning guaranteed meaning

unprecarious, even the cruel
curl of the ear of the dog born into

circumstances. Velvety meaning
silky meaning this makes me think of

creatures who make silk.
Meaning knowing of far off, the realm

of known, having a smooth
soft surface, meaning having. Having

having. Reminiscent. A memory.
An out. Velvet meaning a surface free

from roughness, from ridges
or bumps or irregularities, having

an evenness, a preservedness,
having an evenness, a preservedness,

having an evenness,
a preservedness, like or as a theatre, as

any place blinked
from a windowseat. As the wall

behind the portrait, which goes
and connects to the rest of the house,

to the woodwork and the stairs,
the roof and fence and hill. As the wall,

even, behind the subject of
the portrait. Velvet meaning continuous, without

notice, without occasion for
disturbance. Hard to know what to

make of it—light falls to each point
different. Our world bunched, shot through

with dark, burdens
burned in. We cut slits. Cut and cut

and cut. Sit for
our portraits, stain

our lips. Pray be caught.
Say please, say cheese, say red thousands

of times. Now with head down,
now with arms behind, now with

mouth open. Now with
the whole of you looking out from

within. Be the pink
lining. Be chocolate. Be the bee.

Be that name burned into you.
You are free. Heights sigh inside

cursive pressing slow, this way now.
Forward just a little more, that's it you're

a peach. Assign it, decide it.
I lie flat, so unlike you subject,

and imagine the earth siphoning,
shuttling elsewhere, myself as water

and earth as air, as wicking as
fire as season, as time, and over

the course of it becoming
as true as architecture from which visitors

have been subtracted.
Velvet do you know the pleasure

of creating the space to which
we give body. I think about being that precise

lying here looking up—
what it means to register mostly one's

ending, what it would be
to become the opposite of reaching—

losing your own hand, slipping, liquid
some, falling from, pooling and accumulating

dumbly wherever the hem? I wasn't
until I almost sung. Velvet I couldn't

care less how many albums
you cover, what I want to know is how

one fills one. How long
I might look at something glorifying

the rich pass between radiance
and extinguishing. I'll press a thousand leaves

out of a butterscotch-and-maple-
marbled bolt but pointedly avoid echoing

the living. We're all peculiar
to an I think comforting fault.

Is it fault where I rest,
where I might give in or give.

Is it beneath, is it relevant,
this questioning, this pocket

I'm guarding, the weight
of the planet I keep in my knees—

like a flame for a second.
Velvet I can't imagine you above me.

I hover in front of your
framings, pause atop your eternal cut—

put you on the sensate side
of my hand, which is to say

the under that remembers.
Velvet the world is loose and tipping

and I certify it with a saturated,
jeweltoned ferocity, draw you near until

I look like the wrong side
of something. Velvet bent, a common grass

with slender stems and
narrow leaves, *agrostis canina*, there he is again

the little dog that runs through
what gives us pause, Rhode Island bent, brown

bent, dog bent, velvet bent grass.
Grass for pastures and lawns, that mows

to an even height say for the purpose
of putting. Velvet-textured: smooth. Like

it would feel in the mouth, as
a puree enhanced with cream. My rabbit

was cheap; my pockets
won't speak openly of the conditions

under which they were made.
What matters is the hand. The short soft

dense warp pile.
Use it in a sentence

it determines both syntax and vision.
The longer you look, the deeper it slows.

We roll ropes out of it
and hang them wherever we want to make

a suggestion.
What velvet says keeps us obedient.

Think of fireside, think a fireside seat.
Think of rising by that light, brushing no

story, registering no silky, sunken
plane. Think of abandoning each thought

midsentence over the arms of
the chair, those little rooves the count

of firesides multiplying casually
beneath. Think of being stitched by

the sentence so utterly
as the needle in and out

thousands of times atop the warp,
the weft, the hand checking the slice

of the resulting pile. Think of
a life made up of this multiplication,

of an armchair enough to encase an ever.
Think of the moon shade and the moon pooling

where each moonpoint opened ground
to admit the drawing-down: a drain taking,

we remain velvet-tongued, saying *table it*
over the rush, *look at that* over what's overlooked.

We occupy, edit, table-tent, moon-
headed, humming an ongoing commitment

we've only committed not to quit.
The best velvet banks nowhere for the night.

Texture draw us
back into one place.

Draw the autumn its
certain pictures, ones that establish

what to solve for want.
The landscape spectral behind us.

It reduces.
Step into it, acquire that drape.

Fascinate.
Become subject.

To be subject is to disrupt,
to injure the tender onlooker.

Good luck getting past
the center of the shot. It baits you

neither flame
nor extinguishing.

You call the surface *mine*
as it digs deeper the well sounding

mine mine mine.
As though consenting.

Velvet give me sonorousness.
Leave me rung. Beyond amorous.

I'll travel the longing
until it becomes the dress.

All texture shushed except
that sensation inside raised to what silences.

That black dress exhausts the floor,
its pockets loose and deep. Sometimes

I'm so tired I can barely see a line—
where does us begin. Where are the edges

of my garment. Growing up
velvet announced its patches, burns, future

transparency. One of my favorite days
in the brick building we learned about irony

then wrapped it spare and prayerful
around our necks. Some direction reversed

inside. Hands twitched,
a crystal, a thistle, an image. A syncing

we could live in. A sympathy.
Looking out for some stitching.

All sense crosses the nap, shivering.
Velvet wants at it. Shifts and a rib glints.

Ate once but has waited since.
Walks through us growling for ocean,

for the furthest edges of everything,
taking the shadows, taking the chair, even,

that sits by most windows,
everything but the one leaning by

stained & a rain of words like smokestack,
cherrywood, lipstick. Only that & the crescent

writhing then unwriting itself.
That spot thready, patchy, half-zoned,

nothing at midnight but quickening,
refusing obsidian down to the last glove,

the last rope.
It venoms. Blankets are a laugh.

And halls. Put windows in
darkness spills through. Put an ending on

preface spills out. Line a box with it
and the inside crumples like sage in heat and cold

at altitude. An ear will sensitize
if neighbors bleat, turn silvery and plush as

underside. In stories, the rabbit is
definite, the neighbor lambs a holy numerology.

To put away velvet is to be scraped—
the legs of the girl inside tights, her eyes

the shadow of the dress, the shadow
of the dress the doll she holds, the doll

she holds the carved wood against which
she leans, that wood the whole of the unseen

house, that house the past
and the present, the future beyond her

where we are the yolk of
her face illuminated, fixed on

something else—this is what
we get, inside experience, this portrait of

a girl a couple years after
there was finally a college for women.

What does any doll tell us,
posed invitationally. The new ones

wear their fathers' jackets
over concert tshirts, lapels flowing,

tongues unconstrained. For my name
my parents chose an unpronounceable synonym

for marvel, almost mirage, and so
I pulsed & cursed & kicked. O heavy-ponied

muse, what shade would you call
that scrap tied loose around the sum?

Maybe caramel burned.
The ribbon flips when the girl looks away

to where she's actually called.
As by a carol, a thought almost iridescent,

almost blonde, sleeves sliding open
to reveal arms when you lean. An opt-out.

The feeling of distance like
mink or uninterrupted sleep.

Untangled, rolling out, integral rather
than decimal rather than guttural. For once

we might have both eyes and throat,
to radiate the deepest possible red-tinged

indigo-lit royal violet, to pupil out
sparks to match the bright licks steeped

in the centers of flowering things.
No matter how many histories I scan

I cannot find where permission
comes in. Where it comes, and the meaning

of in. Plainness one face
shimmering drape the other. What's

more a given than a question tipped
between indigo, bruise. What's more

an eye than the well that fills. What's
more clear than our sustained bluetone.

I can speak and speak. Maybe
velvet's backing this attention I'm paying. Maybe

we've been ruined on stories
that progress towards ending. A friend says

this is the hospice of
the world. This would explain.

Lucie died & I went up
trusting information. I trust

velvet's grieving the line. And
everything left stands straight up.

Those heights equally.
I run my hand over grief.

Run my hand over grief.
Feel grief beneath my hands and

keep feeling. The point of grief
is feeling stands us up. The cloth is

continuous, the bolt generous.
The length longer, taller than all of us.

A library arranged
to evoke the idea we should at some point

read everything. A writer reads
and reads then sees something and stops

reading. All writing is reading.
All coats are heavy coats. All seats

bestow support and cage us.
All texture threatens numbness.

See the women in the street
their coats sheening. They say *just threw it on.*

They vow. The vows
stitch the winter through

lesson lesson lesson
every line a title. The world

is gone or I am. Line-
giver. Air crinkle. A crack the maximum.

Oh, this old thing
a ring in the air when you bite it.

Again I circle
what is a vow.

A leap an admission.
Whatever I speak. What

does it offer.
What does speaking offer.

What do I interrupt,
running this hand across

as though to stand it,
as though to counter what has stood.

Eventually words multiply.
I worry number diffuses reason.

Could articulate every shade
in the order they spilled and what would

that extend.
In a vow one name

appears repeatedly.
One leads the other across

the illusory nature of the textile.
The leaps both dream and material.

The spectrum
both promise and question.

It leads.
That's what this is.

The understanding
that in the gorgeous tortures

those flashes
map out something moving.

No colorword
should appear more than once.

What finally is the speaker
to offer and to whom? I keep trying

to get at what happens
when the light hits the cut tips of the nap

and pours off like waterbirth, like
opal, like muscle stretching prismatically

with the blood of one's purest
animal panting. It's living, the illusion.

What we're eager to wear.
A jewelcoat pulsing. Ever thrill

at the structure of a lining
keeping us walking into wind?

The clothes get us
where we're going. I stay with

the absolute
& the possible. The offering.

I find so much looking
away from, I rarely look up.

I promised to delay morning.
Promised to carry the entirety,

every line a title I realized
but did not write. When winter goes long

yes, I possess it. Yes, I can force it.
Yes, I am married to it. I studied at the school

I was offered, found my way
through the trouble. *Yes, my veins resemble.*

Yes, the lines are untranslatable.
I did not study at her velveted feet;

I studied the ground beneath:
That the name of bliss is only in the diminishing /

(As far as possible) of pain. That I had quit /
The quiet velvet cult of it, / Yet trouble came.

My senses tell me I meet myself
anywhere that is soft or not. The line

leads towards naming
but is not the name itself.

Oh, this old thing, I give it to the air
& the year. It passes through the lightest ring

then leaps out ardently.
It knows the directions in which

lines lie, in which lines point.
I give it to the air blinking, cinching, caping.

Upon altars, thrones, the canopies
of high beds it accompanied violent force,

surreal and manifest on the shoulders
of portrait subjects immediate with death.

Its grip an argument of the rules, guard
of the theatre, its curtains and seats, angelic

and profane. I found its intriguing structure
lesbian & throttling. Understood its promise was

consideration, eternal
consideration, consideration both raw

and complexly dyed. Reclining,
hand on crotch, some proposal beyond

hypothesis. *Velluto*, fleecy.
Encyclopedic. Debate-stirring.

A woman walks into a room,
underscores something terrifyingly supreme.

Velvet is the walls is the vault
is the projection is the upholstery is the very

lining of the very carriage.
For every reputation an imitation

where the original keeps
inimitable pile, emblematic, genetic: it was

once *established that both simple and ornate*
velvets could have no fewer than three hundred threads

per ligature and no fewer than
eighteen ligatures (at least 5400 threads), and

must have gold in the selvege, used
to read the type dyes used (De Marinis, 15) and

is thus impossible to study
without studying thoroughly. Admired

for that unpredictable nature
of its shades and nuances. Who was it

who tweeted that the only way
to stay on-brand is to bend. O smooth velvet,

o warp pile velvet, o gold
brocading wefts, Lucca introduced them

to the markets of Europe.
That decorative imagination: *animals run,*

fly, chase each other, shaking
their tails, paws, and manes; the forms

of the plants twist and flex in sinuous
movements; streams gush forth and rays of sunlight

dart swiftly (De Marinis, 25).
Every degree of tension exists

to shift itself. This is
the closest we'll get to wearing

another's effort, underwriting
another's debt. I used to think white

forced the most delicate, painstaking work:
meaning I staked my pain to the white field

& that blinding.
Think of the polychrome velvets

with up to quadruple warps, then
the bas relief types, their different pile heights.

Like hormones' sensitivities
they light up all over the place.

Sobering, black pile-on-pile,
a vision held. Vision, as much about

what's blocked out as what's held.
The center has to have edges, and the edges

have to graduate away from
the subject. A subject has requirements

I accepted long ago.
It dismisses us, and while we might attempt

some pretense of permitting its seat
it is both the seat and the subject. A subject

has requirements. Ask yourself what
you accuse saying *lavish*, what you sink

saying *arabesque*. The drapes
remain heavy, their dark red pears outlining

an endlessness of pears.
Fabric is a fertility, a trigger for displeasure.

Imagery's religious. Examples are
examples, clustering. I hope for moods

like fonts from life before
the internet, italic-matched. The subject

does not ask how another is
or does. A subject knows us, which is why

we choose to pay it.
The pomegranate, the thistle, the center

of the rose. Death left out.
Lamps and laces, vases of vines, vertiginous

sense, trust in metaphor, earnestness,
a commitment to spareness, to choice.

Want & don't synonymously.
Glow, glow promises the complication.

Abstraction promises the abstract motif.
Likeness promises the pomegranate. Design's

irrational but it reasons in terms.
When someone announces *velvet is back*

they mean we've forgotten enough
of the last starvation. Call it bombé or Gandin,

some effect dressed for exposition—
everything trompe-l'oeils, flutter-ends, the lip

of some distant ringing. We rehearse
the transparencies of eras in decompose.

Who knows what's warp, what's
weft. A tiny bird on a blood-red bud,

a Turkish fruit on an unkillable
vine, a betrayal, a trumpet, a heavy-lidded

hungover signal, a horizon collapsing,
a glimpse of the wealth that points roads.

In a dream I saw a dress of velvet
knotted around itself, leaving a keyhole,

an exposure of what it dressed. The color
fictitious as grape juice. Narrative is a dense

tradition, the keeping of it a collective
project. There's the telling, then the holding of

the breath. A texture sticks up, splitting me
not in two but into scatters that seek the outline

of that around which they make
a protective shape. I become the everywhere

rather than the where. A story
I tell myself. I won't write it a second time.

A solid color is more than enough
to express depth and commitment. I see it now,

a path to infinity running straight
through monogamy. Check out her hat

from the fall of 1954. I don't understand
much of what I came out of, these orchestral scores

that kept noses tipped down
to avoid eye contact. All those finishes

reminiscent of interiors, saying: I carry
my property with me, I live within it closely—

every woman photographed or painted
belongs to some club. Designers talk about

a total look
pants and a jacket they're dead.

This is why the sigh—for a minute
something catches, rupture in the sheen.

A permission to set one's wishes out,
carmine red, bluegreendream, outer space

indispensable, counterpoint,
great city, gone plum striking but soft.

The opposite of parent.
So I hesitate to bring simulation up.

Theatres are celebrated
because the seating's rich. We sit back,

observe unequal powers on the stage.
I feel no more secure for training myself

to face it all played out. All
those edges threadbare in opera halls,

rows and rows before
a vanishing point mostly concealed.

When we say masterpiece we mean
even if we have no share in the story we can

watch, and when our watching concludes
we can exit a space in which we have been

for an interval darkly equal.
Goodbye, leaves, goodbye, lines,

when I was younger I was impressed by
the weight of things. The tail of beauty hangs

down, I read myself writing.
Rehearse, rehearse, rehearse, says the mind

endlessly, bingewatch, open
the hatch. The good earth may not

remember us. The seeds
of the quince will not repeat our names.

All the scattered, longshot isolations.
Once, I committed to longhand, wrote out

the call that would return
my husband, my wife. If you

forced open those old windows
the satsuma was growing hard that autumn.

Velvet was more nerve than fur,
more tipped than weighted. More dream

than rabbit, the if-ness of the rabbit
underlined. If eyes cannot forgive, stains

inside. I will not skip from velvet
to drifts. There is nothing like snow

I started sitting at a heavy wooden desk
looking out a large wall of windows at woods.

Deciduous. I was there
for a purpose. Individual leaves popping

out. One of the words I located
was *millinery* which I knew nothing about.

I saw those leaves as clearly
as I had ever seen the streetlight burning

from my bed.
They said, *give.*

They gave.
I decided to marry.

I saw the colors. Saw myself naming
the shades of their insistent vintage. Plural,

expressive, a wave.
I say wave because they were waving.

They spoke of softening.
Their speaking reigning me in.

They said, *give.*
Again for a reason.

Inside a gun.
The kind that says now.

I found myself pointed.
The millinery sobbed. I leaned in,

I listen still.
I left the desk, drove listening to one song.

What results from turning inside out?
Visions are honest, even fictional ones,

and if the next step is to slice
from the thick silk pile, I will shear

what has appeared, mark
the weight of its mirror. I don't cry

as I did. I'd be happy to have learned
this is enough. To say *this is mine,* or more

accurately, this is dying, burning,
radiating, giving, shedding, dropping, passing

forth or away. I wish to square
with the velvet of inside, to sink completely

into the library of my life.
To suggest an honorary stain.

The thing about ink is
it takes us in. I grew up inside woodwork,

the dark tree covering the window
of my room. I grew up to be the tree.

As a teen hid behind it
a blue hand inside my shirt

pulsing with tree. We stayed outside.
Make me bruise, make me prune, make me

blackout, make me coalchute.
Ragey cheek, don't be easily blown.

Hold, winedark one,
hold. Be the needle pointing down.

Always point. Never skim.
Your pointing will carry you. Don't let up.

Ink the field. Spill the secret.
We're all slapping ponytails across

the other shoulder, leaning
stony autumns. I long to feel

in front of the pool. That
pocket cut. I was an acolyte of quiet,

my hand registering itself.
The smoke plumes a way we walk

and walk and walk.
A star almost a burning town

almost a seed wished almost
inspiration for a blossom. There is no

minimalism. Cold within reach
means coating, coating means beneath.

I'd stay in, observing. Or
walk the prairie always, the flowers high

and the river dark. The flowers high
and the river dark and the climb as long

as I remember to the top
of the hill where alone was precise

above the assurance of earth
parted for the Huron I longed to read beside

and sleep myself into.
Praise the darkness of rivers—

I wear the part in my chest,
untouchable and buttoned. Everything

published around me.
Now I lust for what I want, not

what attracts. This distinction
I am cleaved. Beauty is a disruptor;

what we keep disrupts us still.
I comb the world for low, low options,

velvet lining the boxes
in which we lie in so many green hills

of this world.
I am devoted, though I've ceased bowing.

Seeing through numbs
one. There are sightlines.

Against the weight of the city
I want to walk, to well, to sink it all, to

turn all the againsts legible.
The lights going on and off repeatedly.

I'll wear the part of the light
we lost, some before and after simultaneous

in the garment—what's shed, flung
off, a flicker, a dapple, a shine bounced,

an imminent cut, goodbye
previous wholeness, you're scissored.

You become the dress you've sensed.
Why we came up with more than a couple of

words for things. When I still
I am richer, a partial infinity. See that

down/up reset
over the crisis—

which world
would assign us

one another. The word
purpose faults like a fingerprint.

I want to be
the best-voiced question.

As ruinous as oil and
as promising, light tearing itself

all surface and resistance during.
There are glaciers yet, & tones we name

referencing. Mud isn't stone.
Walls aren't grounding. The yet

that edges velvet
conceives of everything.

And and and it turns, and
is available here and and is everywhere

you drag some sense of it. And
unconsciously. And unceremonially.

And the season's tipping, the ruin,
the ruining, the leaving and the feeling,

the slipping and the scaring, the motion
that's undulant, the nightfall the wandering.

And says no matter, no matter,
here swallow another, a blunder an always,

the throat weeps its never.
The truer the book the darker its

crushed-pile spine,
the wider its copper-corseted scar.

The other night
the one beside me asked if anyone

still does monograms, and that
felt sort of violent in the sense of

readers' uncertainties dogeared
onto pages that have risked sequences

of punctuation,
of print. All books, abbreviated:

yes. Every choice
taut cuz it actually is.

What I resent about the image
is that it's done. I almost think

I could become something
in the presence of one. Reverence,

tenses—this painting
has taught me so much. The impact

of four dying blooms
in the foreground of what stuns—

every blackberry, lanternberry,
wildrose and gritted snail and patcheye moth

and split fig and curling pea
and prune-about-to-drop before

the window's reflection
in the surface of the vase. Crass things,

their tiny hope megaphones.
Nothing outside the work. Nothing

is big enough. Someday
a title will touch it—those notes

straining behind the marriage
of what's before us and what's nowhere

to be seen.
When I stand here I think

I should have been a painter,
and then I should continue to stand here,

and then forever is not available
outside the painting. If I squint some

lint gets in between the light
and the way the light is crying.

I'm trying to get the evidence out,
a time before this one tonguing me,

heavier with sediment, dust
weighing in sleeves—the tips of my fingers

against once-close embroidery.
Slant light ricochets keenly. All I remember

is using the word *all* differently.
Now I see every woman I meet:

the spots she touches on herself,
the iridescence, the lip, the piercingness,

the apology. I've been
dragging my point across the fibers

and through those dotted lines.
It's something to be seen and something

to see. I flip
between. This x-ray tendency.

Beneath my ribs a folding file
honks and flexes for that always-autumn,

always-winter place where
I've longed to be the one who could

impress others silently.
I have always conjured something felt

to enter myself.
The truth about hidden boys is

girls are charged with seeing
and it's catching up to me. Velvet catches

all it catches
a fresh ancient, a neon iciness,

a bruised birth, a pristine ruinousness,
an untouched open book, a tarnished gilt sword

unremoved from the chest
of the wearer, a barely-tied robe on

an ever-descending stair, a spent
untested seat, a throat opened to the cold

speaking warmly, the stained pillow,
the straps of the desert threatening to slip

like rain. In this world I have been
a tiny hued box edged in grosgrain

dyed postapocalyptic sunset.
Plunk me on cement and bang

I contextualize!
Is velvet always a box,

always a dress, always a threat.
Is velvet always something on velvet,

never touching ground,
always precarious feet lest the bottom

rub off and go lost from the hands
that would pass it. Such a lock, this long

airless moment. Like the plum
named for the elephant's heart, ten times

the bite, its coralline-to-scarlet flesh
gummed against the leather, more abrupt

than summer, more terror-filled.
Silky weaponry, final baptism, robin's egg

coffin, burnt new flame,
kiss extinguishing, a button to close

a lid on a cameo, a cameo to open
the throat of a woman, the throat of a woman

to scissor the institution that
celebrates her finely while denying her exactly.

I can't fit all the language through. Run
a button in, buttonhole edges threaded neat.

Your legs are not your own,
lest you think you've solved the problem

of how you'll leave the room,
its framing and permitting suggesting

something about freedom in restraint,
lightheartedness in contract, the endlessness

controlled by that knot at your waist.
We'd all like to say we conquered the fold,

to toss on something exquisitely cut,
something that had a needle pulled through it

one thousand plus one
thousand times. A line over a line

an asterisk, a pass
on the underside. At the sleeve a notch

edged, the thread so dark
it reads roses or shadows of stars.

These confusions heal us
has been my experience. I don't know

whose arm does the work,
the difference between what I glimpse

and what I take in. Again
an urge to rip bread & consume—

I thought I knew all I wanted
then I stopped breaking lines, tucking them

under and bringing them up
again like swimmers gasping. In the interim

a stroke, a question.
I never got my time alone.

I wear an undone color.
I want an other to come, to ruin out

and in for them.
I intend a love of ruin.

See how expensive. See how
resisting. Velvet gifts what nothing takes.

Verdigris, goldenrod, labradorite,
mud-shot, carbon, blood-bent, foil of

the forest, goldwing, scarab, firefly,
neon at noon, darkest corner of night.

In another life my hair might
have been a streak of burgundy to neon red

to quince to pink. I might have
walked out against lesser saturation into

the lines my own legs made.
But I learned the back of eyelids, a solid field.

Which is to say that which stands out
stands up and away from its own beginning

constantly. Which is to say
the constant in it is the direction of

up and away from all
surface. Which is to say a cost.

The woman with the slit
she draws you in because she cannot

be drawn. Her dress
is an acknowledgment. The woman

in bruised fig silk velvet
is gone. See how the light lights her

as though she's already art?
Art is gone. Gone is solid. The jacket

is an elegy for beauty. Beauty
an elegy for itself. Yes, the fabric

is impossible. I wear knowing down
until it shines. Shadow of mink, then mink.

Night of fig, then fig. I keep
coming back to the word *themselves*—

that plural mess that almost
possesses. Sometimes I put something on

on some behalf.
Behalf is a word I do not

understand. Each of us is taken
the garment acknowledges. We will be palmed,

moved through, moved
and moved and moved, weighed down

by something dark and cut. I am
ready to admit I mean to coax what comes

until distance is the conversation
and the language of the conversation.

I mean to take the dialogue in
skin beneath bodice. Velvet two-tone it.

As a hand comes out
from between an institution's curtains

to wave then remove itself.
I do not permit the world my body just

a portrait. A safe
place to store a ring. That ringing

caught, permanent.
Paused, taking the fire in.

A wreath hung, rough ribbon
wound around magnolia, lichen.

We circle what slips
trying to live in a world.

Some other verb.
Fire rises and I bank before its face:

give the us of us,
recognize. There is

no else.
Velvet give us

our emptiness.
Forget neither end.

That crease beneath the iron.
Those thoughts, permanent. Try

to press out fault, it brightens.
No mirage, just what takes where eye

marries horizon, makes
a final line. It's not that I can't hold on

it's that I won't—
the floor, the walls, the space

between here and the ceiling
do for real. My job is to pass.

Nothing helps you go
somewhere you don't pick up

and go—the full room
impossible to look into, that rustling

something catching on itself.
To perceive the tongue of velvet,

silence. To register
the staining sheen of the nap,

courseness. To realize give,
ungivingness. It's too easy to reference

animals we collar, to liken
domestications to art. I won't say you echo

when what you repeat evenly
barely imagines us. I'm feeling out

where I might sit—
trust velvet to argue it for me, to

clear my path of argument.
I do not want to be guarded

by my seat—just pronounced.
Two planes intersecting behind,

permanently, greyly,
the only permanent cloud matching

a permanent point. I am
torn in intimacy, demanding

a point from which to face out,
not a point into which to vanish.

I want no horizon
closer than my ability to think.

Inside sit almost still, gather
myself. Walls, may you find one another

at ninety degrees behind
the construction I trust cross-kneed,

may you score that hatched glow
behind the well-worn arms on which I lean.

Allow me these arms leaned.
I am old enough to know chairs revise us,

upholstery deceives, we situate
and retreat in corners because bones

fail to solidify. Give me
a chair that is honest I may never

move my tongue again—
give me a beauty that argues my limits

I will save for it frantically.
A story to live up to so I might.

A place to sink
and I'll survive—

some impossibility hitting
skin and bone, touching ongoingness.

Lay that alongside, wear it
slightly, and I'll begin to identify,

bend toward, squint and scry,
an observer dissolving in observing,

a student graduating in studying,
these ever-bent fibers erasing what I

do not perceive to involve
me. The chair has always felt me out—

a well, a welling, a drop,
a spot we keep obviously.

Clean out a closet, there's
nothing but room in it. A note

on a post-it
on the frame.

Not everyone talks
it out, the uprush of a woman

tacked & spoken of & raped
& tried against her aspiration to live.

It's not sexy, any of it.
One can't sit just off the road

hair parted severely on one side,
the flaps of some heavy maroon bell-legs

soaking up light like spilled wine
and not shout we're fucked, cloud-lungs,

we're fucked, rock-dirt altars,
severely & intimately. A full-volume

yawp from the cracks.
Velvet take my legs I pray.

Give me a world they're permitted.
Something to feel into I can stand. Give me I.

The bodies of women
try and try and try. Unlike the still life

I do not name all that is.
I just try. I cannot turn from the thought

or help but rehearse the shades
pulling themselves over us—copper gloss,

iridescent bronze, brandied raisin,
singed persimmon, amber-auburn, snake-

scaled apricot, ombre grey-gold
canary stormdust—each pronounces, lets

as easily as a spaghetti strap
from a hanger lacking teeth.

It haunts me, understand—
velvet's articulate where I am not.

Over & over my arm seeks the inside
of a slow honey sleeve heavy enough to confirm me.

Golden hour, red sunset,
saffron cigar, faded sable, cracked topaz,

mustard rust—every bolt I conjure
backed with silk that is wet, that is dark, that is

stained or snagged, its ribbon-edge
singed. If she weren't spilled gold what

would we see. If she weren't
burned or strewn or gilt. If she weren't

closed to us as though
reachable only as the story.

Ready to sleep.
I fell for women because I could read.

Because women were sleeping
and I wasn't, because women were speaking

and I wasn't, because stories
were telling to me. I fell for what they gathered

and kept gathering. I believed.
A velvet knot loose for its own self,

a stillness requisite for a vision,
an antler growing before a mirror so interior

it's almost platinum-lit,
throwing silver on what stands before it.

I fell for women because I could read
and the more I read the less I hurried. I could be

visions only infinitely.
I could duplicate the velvet book

pull it out hand it over unflinchingly
the register beyond me glowing like fruit

the camera can't stand,
the light throwing off its very image

run off some cliff on all fours,
staggering up jeweltoned verticality.

As exquisite as tonal beading
on the shoulders of a waterfall jacket,

its impossible tone-on-tone embroidery.
Something articulates itself outside an alphabet:

the ceiling in the white room
above me, the pipes cross a shape that says

kite. I see a kite thought, I see
a window fact. My spine moves

impulses, gives a bit. I have
gone velvet waiting for a sign, that I will be

met not by seeking but
by a similarly weighty hand, by pitch

and depth of hue, be shadowed
equally. All those hours I looked for more

doors, keeping in mind desire
for white blankets on dark beds.

Longed for stains to join myself to.
I think I require proof others too refuse

to laugh when laughter is inaccurate,
recognize the evening we are dressing for

is undoing every night. In some eyes
those threads spell it. Velvet is that waving,

that wedding. I look for it
since blackleaves opened beneath my pupils,

shook at what they met.
When Lucie died they wrote about

the radiant girl from Maynard Street
who cut class to go smoke in the park.

I remember myself taking it all out
to the hills that offered sightlines, jealousies.

It sounded like my own hair I was cutting,
the way those trees dropped their interference

some months so I could see
clear across the river. The poet

decided to become a poet
in the middle of algebra. I gave over

to numbers resonant with the emptiness
of my dead father-hole, mother-hole. Nothing

was one or two.
All numbers lied fiercely.

You walked past bricks.
Revise, revise, revise demands

the poem, demands the publisher.
Retry, retry, retry demands the equation.

The poem does not arrive
at a destination. It cuts until it opens

for something stranger. We wove
our hands through each others' hair rejecting

everything we could conceive of
to reject, sparking and finishing unendingly.

It is the texture of the paper
on which I weigh, against which I sound

a namecheck. I want to go
archaic, I whisper to the material wall,

to the maternal well. Only steel
survives the winters and the stake is the line

and the line is the stake mattering
as it's held out above its drop. No series

of words is neutral. You
slipped out of the Rust Belt so you could

break things numerously.
Let's not gloss over the gorge

in gorgeous. I too believe in vows,
in the gorges they scan for the other side of

a future city. The absence of teacher
figuring texturally. Something strict in all

ornament, its ever-specific
insistence. To live in a red velvet room,

to hear as one hears inside.
I'm watching the eyes of girls eyeing the world

as it passes through them.
Lacrimal, threatening meniscuses. See

the mirror spend us. See
the threadbare chair, think how gorgeous

because there's still an us
to glimpse it. Velvet charges, we close our lids.

The truth is I have kept the world
white so it might command. Sought a match

for the degree to which I can
be commanded. Why I could not see marriage

without velvet.
I am as stark as the stone we repeat

over, over for every
unrepeatable word. I do not know

why others do not reject
most of what passes: I want less

so I will sense who I might be.
What calls me into sumptuousness

is the promise it'll just be us.
The whole of the sensory gamut.

Skin static.
Against the chest

it pays a whole attention,
rapt. I'm freed to meet it every

where I am.
What calls me in

is an infinity of feeling
awakening in the *fine* of skin.

In-ness. Feeling like sleep.
I'm eager to give in, communed.

To be whatever sea.
To pass out of us, to be known

broadly & intricately, outfitted
in knowing and known, the silk velvet

on shaved skin of known,
the ethers racing to engulf the whole

of known, the spectrum of
sunset and flame in it, honey and indigo

takeover. It only works
in heat-shimmer & ether, that combo.

In stone it's a joke.
Looking at the ring, a dragging.

Sumptuousness is something
between us & this. A cut that swings,

a severance. Velvet-nap &
rocks in glasses, edges tipped to clink

off-topic. Sumptuousness
is the off-hour guttering us.

The sky's cooler hues debuting
a new radius of thoughts. Sumptuousness says

why think about it. Thoughts
are narcissus. A dress is a toddy just hot enough

to pass into oneness.
Feels good going on &

then we drop in
to what has abandoned us.

The before pool that had us fooled,
something mirage or image we felt surely

& then peeled out of, exposed.
Not everything reaches in. Not everything's

orgasmic ratchet. Only narcissus
is narcissus, & it blooms at the turn, rain-awake

& translucent, stabbing.
I go to sleep knowing. I go out singing.

I know everything known
is velvet's sentence: I stand

inside myself.
Handle alone. The land-ripples

promise a life in silk's reflections,
in the distractions & ethereals, philo-

sophical, theoretrical, pastel & abstract,
as light as chiffon that exists to make us think

about nipples, not of hunger,
but of nipples, and of the state of feeling

accelerating our insides towards us
from outside, almost religiously, almost

conceptually, as when we're moved
by art to some impossibly vertical & dizzying place

where everything touches.
Through the hills that shape snakes,

a fine hand. A top dropped on a chair
pools in itself, its own future memory fast against

the seat.
Synonyms multiply, become

stupendousness. Fabric acts on one
as music does, setting molecules bonking.

Every feeling seeks a dress
& an undressing. Every tone of voice

an imbued hue twin.
A rainlessness. A silk dancing out its laws.

A row of buttons we say fuss
holds fast its warmth to the limit

drawing the sidewaist, the napedrop,
the sleeve. I regain a self comforted as a locket.

A monogamy a surround.
What I know is I needed to get married

& couldn't explain.
That failing was a hem

I only recognized after the climb.
A beautiful shredding. I married her

windswept. For the long autumn's
prosaic burnish & the stark winter's hearthflame.

For colors richer than their namesakes
offering themselves to capture, to claw.

I've been called the spitting image
of another who'd no sense of looking up

from his book & pushing his eyes
through the streams of falling golden motes

to enter the space
through which the day was falling.

I can't play the part of color:
I can remember that it will drop.

Thanks dad.
Sometimes when I drive my car

I know a presence, a defiant eros,
live as an elegy. I've managed my terms.

Stones do.
Accused of being fixed, permanent,

the lucid simply listen.
Stones are their own—

that fact the cushion.
The one who sleeps through these questions

intends never to divorce.
I lean against our light-bent headboard,

pressing into it the curve of a spine.
If I had one minute I'd spent it retelling

this place with fan turning,
window open, familiar linen, my hair

twirled by my hand back over
a shoulder, and the reassurance of

beauty behind me
convincingly. Before me the pulp

of trees inked.
Emboss leaves, draw them

into a circle, wire them around
a ring, hang them upon a door. *Accept*

is a verb. Line boxes
then monogram. Make a thing of

that privacy. Velvet is not a pillow
it is a leaf upon a pillow. Velvet is not

a saved swatch it is futurity.
Down the center of the long table

let no one say your name—
let no one pretend. See the drape

of the pool, speak the nature
of the water. I return burning and accept

I have had my visions
and the season's turned again.

Monogamy
wearing the garment.

Not just hanging it
in a room then remembering.

Committing to remembering
less of the story, more of the space it takes up.

I don't go out scanning
for answers. They start where I am.

I pulled up
alongside someone who understood.

Monogamy accepting the cut
and living within as one lives one's name.

The garment repeats the body,
a voice close, a heat close, a hold.

A memory of itself.
I know I will have come home

when I cease telling in excess.
Let someone else remember me.

The pool accepts. We
gather at its edge. We enter it

over and over, keeping ourselves
wet. I have entered the conversation,

we suggest. I am the carrier
of the pool, I am kept by the pool, I am

gathered by the pool, I am enveloped
by the pool, I live inside the pool, I cannot exit

the pool, I am sleeved and legged
by the pool, shaded by the pool, hued

by it, I cannot escape the pool,
I have committed to it, I have married the pool,

given myself as a body to
a form, as a skin to an inside. I have

given myself as a skin to an inside.
What we measure is how hard inside's rubbed—

the glint of that waft, weft crossed,
and what future finds the shine evident.

The story of what left.
I envy its enunciation, its refraction

off the bend, its narration
shoulders readable beneath tailoring.

What the tailoring reads,
confirms. The rise of the neck

from it. In the narrative I was
the ruin creased into the nap. Never taught

to say my own name. I moved
into room after room wondering why I

loved the walls of them,
why anything vertical stood. Velvet

to create the window folding
one's auburn draping about the throat.

Lucie we ache like a slit.
That day my dress had a high one

& I hiked up while behind me
she gathered all that had dried that long summer.

A long and private walk, the two of us
& the officiant & the witness breathing hard

& speaking little. I'd stuck
a ribbon in the backpack & at the top

tied that horizon-hammered argent crush
around the bleached-out bouquet. Ever stair,

ever ascent—scrubflowers
gone to seed shot through with glare

gone chalk, strawblonde against
the end of the land & the year. The ocean

silenced below &
we joined the silver rule,

pinned to it
as though garment. Took turns

holding those flowers as we
read from Patti and Richard and Agnes

and Nicole and Agnes and
Richard again. The wind was loud

and most of those it carried dead.
The whole time. I cannot name the flowers;

I did not see them alive.
Everlasting in our devastation

for them we stand up
putting the sum in a ring.

We have nothing. Nothing keep us,
nothing clean us, nothing hold us here

but the prongs of these selves:
we are our hands for the ceremony,

already passing through one another
like dye or time. I could call conjured blue

a shade like wave.
I could call shadows armor plum

or anchor bruise. Oh
to resuscitate. Oh child and parent, oh

perfume hanging, oh strands
crossing one's face in the wind.

Oh after.
Oh through oh break out.

To play the register. To
tie back that rule to use every word

the moment it's learned
a hand in one's hair mastering its own knot.

To be intimate with all we haunt.
A familiar pair of hands twisting oneself

into brutal soft rope.
To animal a world inside. To solstice it.

To live shedding the flowers
to the paper via proper names. To shepherd

that lining, its reminding—
little gathers, little stitches, needle-pulled

bunting-blossoms knotted small,
bursting pearl. Somehow sentiment.

Whatever we make
a pocket. The thought, bias-cut atop

a wire stem, the petals dimpled
and twisted over flame-warmed tools,

coaxed into permanence.
A little spent at edge, as with the original,

letting something go
even as we pin it. Voila, the velvet

viola, hydrangea, delphinium,
forget-me-not. Chamomile hums along

a loose bud spray, a berry cluster,
the raisins, a small apple and its leaf.

Morningglory, starflower,
dogwood, boudoir flower. Drag a velvet chair

before the house the house
is less for it. Bring it in, it overpowers.

So with the demi-crown
sprung around the millinery: the hat

shrinks the woods, the world,
the open mouth of the admirer. What is

the point of a chair if it's not
inherited. What is any knot if it unknots.

Defend your knottedness!
Not cognac but burnt sugar. Not

opera mauve but permanent
geranium lake. Not quinacridone

but prune but redbud, tulipwood.
Not sunglow but inchworm but icterine, but

iceberg, but hooker's green.
Papaya whip but aureolin. Bisque

but linen but jasmine. Wild strawberry
but upswell red but fire opal but ultra red.

But heatwave but glaucous
but orange soda but flame. Cider syrup

but desert daybreak but wheat
but fallow but eggshell. Crème de pêche but

cornsilk but silver chalice.
Not silver chalice. Silver chalice

but thistle. Thistle but volt but wenge
but winter sky but wintergreen dream but aero

but ao but platinum. Not wine dregs
but dark lava but dark liver but black chocolate

but caput mortuum
but absolute zero. The run is fast,

the tonality full-blown. All the promises
sumptuous. Rare flowers, moths large as mouths

in motion. Straight up
dark tonality. Not tonality but

center. Not center
but bottom. But wellshaft,

but voice.
Shooting up.

I long to go
having destroyed the white granule,

an antler
commanding a tine split.

Velvet over bone, over thought.
Velvet conducting fog, conducting texture.

Fine rain touches, changes
my temperature. The velvet book unwrites

the touching.
I am inside. Velvet run up

across the breast around
the neck and twisted under the pit.

Velvet the shoes and the evidence,
the bones, the choices. Velvet could I

call this curtain, keep my hands
between the crack of the curtains

and call it completion, holding
that part. Velvet the sheen's rubbed

off the pincushion. Velvet no one
remembers to whom the necklace belongs

here at the back of the bottom
tray of the box. Velvet, lingo of assuredness

and heavy hems,
swinging at the knees. Keep me.

Open your lidded passage
to reveal an impression. Velvet beckon

and defend. Leave ribbons
in a heap over the lamp, tie nothing

but the thought to its pointing.
Enunciate the syllables between

those moments we won't. There is
a depth to this, eraser, collapser, reductionist,

there is rationale where you have
minimized it. There is, there is, says velvet,

arms to sleeve, rings to box,
cosmos in thread, schools of thought of

stars of libraries like languages like
bodies we can literally walk. There are

needs. Take two ends
and loop them through one another,

close the gap between:
the velvet knot will keep itself,

the velvet slit will speak of
its opacity, the velvet drape will

orate on organic forms just as
a parrot tulip will rhapsodize eventually

re: the earth, the leafpile,
the shadow scent, the protective aspect,

all the rest. Only a known
can point. Against shine, only matte.

The one who made the rings
hammered the metal then stabbed asterisks

all the way around, twice.
The vision keeps me distinctly

as any fiber standing above its field,
sheared neatly, weighed with remembering

shades and hues, the relationship
between warp and weft, straight line and bent.

Here reaches up.
Here, ceremoniously.

We are the stillness revolving
around the life that evolves between

yester and member, between
days and revise. The deep dark ache

of the couch catches me.
The deep dark ache of the couch

catches me. Roll everything
before. Under wonderwater. A woman

in her underwear.
A velvet inside matching her.

I wish the world had some
steepness to it not just severity.

Things beaded
stored in the dark. A neat shoulder

in chocolate plum, in
burgundy fudge. Almost a language,

almost a decision,
the mirrors darkening in pleasure.

Bow down, rivers, she comes
in studs, in tones, with emphasis,

irreverent and covered in subtle
metal, her ring a weapon, the point on it

a thing alone.
Switch her spotlight switch her meaning.

I took the ring out of the box
and gave it. Accepted its twin, mixing up

the prepositions of the line.
It was all very quiet. Elk, pelican, a silk.

I felt myself rising up through the surface
like a text going vertical, reaching past italic

for plainface, for capital.
I felt myself inside myself filling myself out.

This is what it means to breathe:
I have been feeling an absence out

that's now absent. Over
and over, out's existed everywhere.

When I slept, the sheets wrinkled, white.
Operatics of bronze on October Sundays.

I felt myself ready to sleep again.
When I wake the velvet will register,

pointing me.
I will be able to wear it.

I will palm a warm box
with two grooves parallel

beneath an emblem.
as if knowing the ridgebump

of some soothing skull
under fur. How, says the bone's shape.

I realized what I was.
I have not transformed but I have

been surrounded.
Stones are worth keeping, whatever

keeping means—
we bring the world in. Set

and pronged
it fits. A vision.

How to feel past any limit of hands.
Go out every autumn among the last flowers.

They have already dried
in the field. Have already given.

Claim them between hands
you've slowed, between breaths stowed for

other directions.
Put a hand down upon

that which you are confirming
and confirm it always, darken it with

confirming. What's crushed
is most honest. I remember fingers

the texture myself.
If all things I begin begin

in the mouth
and the muscle of the mouth

is a rough, napped thing
that scratches, laps, bends, points

and goes rogue, and the root
of that muscle is swallowed, and

the swallow is but one act
of the unconscious self in the moment

of registering, that swallow
is the beginning retracing its own root,

and there on the roof of the mouth
it rests we'd say docked, just before unhinging,

before going to work undoing
the settled molecules, before applying itself

to the task of dragging its tiny,
sensate hooks over another hooked surface

and coaxing or forcing said hooks
in a direction, just before changing the direction

of what minute invisible piles make up
the giant pile, the texture of the air, the zeitgeist,

just before aiming
for the zeitgeist. What if I could

imagine this
the next step of velvet.

What comes up comes from
somewhere. What we commit

we live in as a room.
Rooms open into one another.

No one knows where beauty
comes from and the longer one chases it

the more world it finds to hide in,
to open through, to commit us to. Rooms

open into one another.
I write a line with something in my eye.

Velvet's what gives,
then what's giving. I feel everything

where before just palm.
I take in the space as it appears.

Take in the room, blooming
for my hand. I could have said no

more precisely all along.
Velvet I see it. You've come.

The combination of yes and no
running through one another as

electric blue sheen through
antique copper-red-rust gleaming.

We have no word
and reaching for it are frozen.

That's what shows
in the picture. The need for a word.

What if velvet was the initial,
the prompt, the first vision of all we called.

What if this dress was the calling.
What is it that has me by the throat.

The poem is fascinated
with continuousness, insurance,

untouchability. The cyclical
governing of its argument. And yet

its horizon's only
ever us. Both sides can be almost.

All work wakes, dreams,
wakes again. The question of form

is the question of how to stay
and then how to allow for drift. In front of

the house, one narcissus,
a white loophole, its fragrance.

On the mantle
the helichrysum, the chrysanthemum,

the strawblade, the lanternberry.
Something burned then burned out,

the whisper of
its first self. I was

fire, I was violet,
I was radish-top, I was rain-on-a-rose.

I hang the bells on the nail
and I wait, thinking: this ribbon.

I used to think an album
opened, or would. Believed images had

their subjects in front of them.
Now I count scarlet and marigold plumes

laid above an indigo plane,
trust dark paintings. The lines

blurred between figures, smoking
all proportions. What might have been

a single person
now a moving history for a frame

and in that frame
the flux suggesting.

There is poetry in the choice.
In the summary there is only what

we take away, not
the original language. The original language

does not open into other languages,
into our own terms. I am the soft charcoal

cursive of the blooms
that are left: there's no sway that will

move the flower,
its throat damning and open.

I needed to know
the dark turned, or would.

Needed something
platinum in the midst of ink,

of opinion. Deliriousness,
not convincing. When I think back

I see a girl who believed
what is was. Continuousness.

The bolt always generous.
I was raised in a house in which

things were held up for pinning.
Women communicated numbers

over the phone, their marriages
amber lowering, changing hue behind glass.

Each sewed and sewed and sewed.
I begged a bolt of blackest black and a pattern

but the skirt went unmade.
I've always needed to know the dark

turned, and would, so chose
a dropped shoulder and a magnificent slit.

Soles pocked and scarred.
Inside the starpoints a buildup.

Inside silver a tarnish.
Inside radiance exhaust, exhaustion.

Inside an eye a pool. I needed
to know the dark turned, and would. That

wood would reveal oil, that
oil would give to glistening. That

the leather into which I sunk
would return, not just host, the shape.

That the room for sleep
would be the room where I would stitch

many things. That the insides of sleeves
would feed an excitement of limbed-ness.

With this ring I
thee wed the first

person says
to the second.

With the operative
word, the highlight

in front of its carrier.
Frost at first light, the path

prismatics.
I will always think back

to the river I walked
to the first place I breathed.

I needed to breathe.
To see that a vow would both hold

& move quicksilver through.
To know liver glinting in lakedark,

lamplight glowing in let-gold.
That strawgrass would bleach-glow

on the hills, that phosphorescence
would turn in the waves, that fire would

unwrite mountains where
we knew each other and knew nothing

of each other, where we knew
nothing and waited as though still in

the water, soaked continuously
by its shadows, buoyed in its tones. As though

its tones. I needed
to know. That my sign was

seeking, not caught. That
my life was meeting. I needed to feel

into moving, into the edge
that's forever testing. The man

across from me said many times
stay, let the bed settle, let the water clear.

Water is always clear
carrying its focus, focusing what it finds,

finding faces in its surface,
watching them come, watching itself go,

less in search than moving freely.
Many mistake what they see in me

for me.
Water knows, travels its totality

turning totality out
each inch. I know it yet

in the skin I walk
it registers as thought.

I reach for velvet
thinking it will complete feeling.

The entire project.
In velvet I can sleep.

I know what I want
to remember, and I know what I want

to repeat. *We kiss*
a needle considering available fabric.

I stud. I stick. Most
language is broken. Most lines break.

Velvet sucks everything up,
ruptures, flashes it, flows like current.

However difficult, however luck,
that shine strokes and strokes and strokes.

Here, it says.
Here now, now now.

Button up. Our eyes
marvels, murmurs, animals

descended from god knows what.
Velvet pants open-mouthed, pained

and paining.
You feel it coming in headlong.

Its gleam bloom.
Are consumed. Finger velvet's message—

none of us belong.
Here, living thing, frantic formal

performance, let's
drape about us that longest promise—

velvet was leaning,
tall to long then lengthening.

Velvet was the lengths to which
all of us went, cinching us as though

vertical slits. Velvet
was mean as the meanest thing and

meant what it said—strung up
trusts. Tripped us. Watched us turn

toward orienting light
and let itself drop down heavy, singing.

Velvet knew our concerns
and argued irrelevance. Claimed

to have come from nowhere
when in fact it could not be worn out.

I long all year for months
when it's obvious how cold the world is

and spare on the inside,
just the pressing of one almost sensation

to another, a pile absorbing
the fact of a hand. If that is yearend

then the space around that
registering, the line inside lighting

the space some carry
for lines. Watch this ripple, some

sense bending, some sensing
confirmed and tumbled and burnished

and hammered into
that once and always result. Velvet

I put my hand out.
I have seen the words, all of them

yours. I know them
by heart. I have walked along

knowing I was supposed
to walk, to let walking clarify me.

We all need some edge
with our tenderness. Some finity.

To pin something winged
to the black nap, to bear witness

then swear the incomparable moment.
I was supposed to swear before the others

all along. To become
that swearing independently.

I am still becoming the swearer,
feeling out what we mean by after.

Still repeating after another.
Velvet I am not holding out.

Every word I commit
the murmur runs through me.

I am free from the beauty
I read and read and read. I said

free. I am free from
the beauty I read and read and read.

NOTES

A few italicized threads in the text are sampled from Lucie's poems: *we were supposed to die out...* (9) from "Domestic Mysticism," *Am lean against...* (14) from "Am Moor," *That the name of bliss is only in the diminishing...* (30) from "The One Thousand Days," and *We kiss* (91) from "Elective Mutes."

A couple of additional italicized threads in the text (32) echo Fabrizio De Marinis' *Velvet: History, Techniques, Fashions* (Idea Books, 1994), the only survey of velvet yet published in English.

The speaker of this poem does from time to time slip into and out of her own self-consciously italicized language, sounding out samples of language from the archive of voices that live in her head. None of these moments owe debts to specific source texts.

ACKNOWLEDGMENTS

Profound spectral gratitude to those journal and magazine editors who ran excerpts from and conversations about this poem in the final months leading up to its publication, including Rachel Contreni Flynn and Kirun Kapur at *Beloit Poetry Journal*, Luiza Flynn-Goodlett and Michal 'MJ' Jones at *Foglifter*, and Jojo Lazar and Addie Tsai at *Anomaly*. Thank you too to Margot Douaihy for the brilliant cross-talk over *Scranton Lace*.

Blinding scattershine to Margaret Holley, who first put Lucie's poems before me as an undergraduate writer; A.V. Christie, who taught me what an emotional arc is; and Alice Fulton, whose nudges have moved me towards a marriage of maximalist and minimalist impulses for more than twenty years. The now countless writers of Scribe Lab, who saw every one of these lines as I combed out the endlessness in my mind, and in particular Lani Scozzari, whose own books of days came into focus in parallel with this one, and made its scale scrutable to me. My colleagues and beloved students at UC-Davis, who have offered me their morning faces, their questions on post-its, and a lamplit treehouse office among flowering branches. The friends and family who made so many deeply felt offerings during the four years I spent writing and revising, most especially Anne Farris, Caren Halvorsen (who, among other things, taught me enough about lightboxes to help me shoot the cover), Christy Heron-Clark, Rachel Nelson, Sarah Pape (who voiced the thought about the hospice of the world), Monica Rico, Karma Waltonen, Gretel Wandesforde-Smith, Kate Washington, and Elise Winn. Elizabeth Bernstein, Mary Coss, and Angela Morris for the month of dinner conversations that bent my life permanently. Julie Andrews for inspiring my personal understanding that marriages should have themes. Richard Siken for putting the rock-solid stuff behind me that I needed in order to carry this through the years I was writing it. Everyone at Point Reyes Books, the Woodland Public Library, the ShangriLee retreat, the Marina Flat, and all of the other refuges throughout the golden state where I find myself both utterly at home and moved in silent moments to reinvent the world. In Cahoots and Writing Between the Vines. The good people of Cornerstone Press and the Portage Poetry Series—publisher Dr. Ross Tangedal, Carolyn Czerwinski, Grace Dahl, Ava Willett, Natalie Reiter, and Sophie McPherson—for their respective intricate labors and for offering this work the fastest yes of all time. And, of course, and most especially, Lucie Brock-Broido, for giving me a different Pittsburgh to come from than the one I left.

The shorthand I use when describing what this poem is about has to do with queer commitment and changeability, and with how yes and no are more dedications to or functions of each other than they are true opposites. So too do great love and grief pour out entangled ring-harmonics. Lucie's death in the spring of 2018 and the subsequent outpouring of remembrances of her and her velvet salon in Cambridge were the spark of this poem, but it wouldn't feel right to release it into the world without also saying goodbye and good release to the friends, mentors, colleagues,

ACKNOWLEDGMENTS

and community members who were lost while I was turning myself inside out to bring this poem to completion during the first year of the pandemic, including Taryn Belmonte, who was the first person in the world to read me as queer, Sarah Schuetze, whose wisdom anchored both my poetry and my soul during my Michigan years (and whose trust in ritual unfolds in my body every time I put on a string of beads), and Kirk Stoller, whose translations of my private languages means I will never feel alone (or brotherless) again in this lifetime.

This poem is for KS and RS, who I hope will meet sitting next to each other in the audience in the next life.

RAE GOUIRAND is also the author of two collections of poetry, *Glass is Glass Water is Water* (2018) and *Open Winter* (winner of the Bellday Prize, 2011), the chapbooks *Rough Sequence* (winner of the Keystone Chapbook Award, 2023), *Little Hour* (winner of the Swan Scythe Chapbook Contest, 2022), *Jinx* (winner of the Summer Kitchen Competition, 2019), and *Must Apple* (winner of the Oro Fino Competition, 2018), and a short work of nonfiction, *The History of Art* (winner of The Atlas Review's Open Reading Competition, 2019). Her work has appeared in *American Poetry Review, Bateau, Beloit Poetry Journal, Bennington Review, Boston Review, Conjunctions, Crazyhorse, Foglifter, The Iowa Review, jubilat, The Kenyon Review,* the *Lambda Literary Poetry Spotlight, Michigan Quarterly Review, [PANK], Quarterly West, The Rumpus, Spinning Jenny, Under a Warm Green Linden, VOLT, ZYZZYVA,* two volumes of the *Best New Poets* series, *Please Excuse This Poem: 100 New Poems for the Next Generation, Queer Nature: A Poetry Anthology,* and many other journals and anthologies nationwide. She leads several longrunning independent workshops in northern California and online, including the cross-genre workshop Scribe Lab, and lectures in the Department of English at the University of California-Davis.